Welcome to 7 Simple Steps How to Create a WordPress Website

1. Selecting a Domain

2. Selecting a Hosting package

3. WordPress Quick Install

4. Setting up Your WordPress

5. What's your niche?

6. Who is your audience?

7. Social Media Optimization

About Me

Named top blogger under 21 by PR web thanks to my personal blog, NickThrolson.com. This platform lets me express myself and help others grow and expand their business, making it a place for working together as a group and as friends.

Specialties: Web design, WordPress, Social Media Management, Affiliate Marketing, PPC, PPV, Email, Media Buys, CPA, Lead Generation, direct response marketing, SEO, SEM, Public Speaking, Toastmasters,

1. Selecting a Domain.

There are many domain registrars online – some of the best ones are the most straight forward ones; I personally like www.godaddy.com but you can also use namecheap.com or any other plethora of domain name registrars out there.

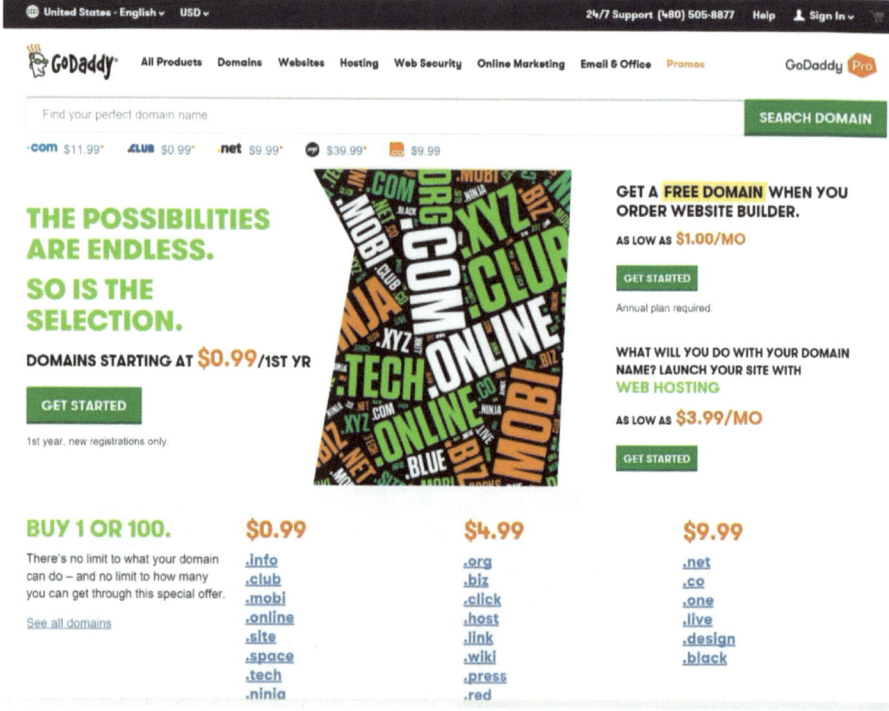

So to begin to go to Godaddy.com and you will be presented with the web page above.

Selecting a Domain Name Tips

- Keep it short
- Stick with a .com
- Don't purchase More Than One Domain
- Sleep on it
- Brainstorm
- Easy to remember

1. Selecting a Domain.

In the search bar, type in your desired domain name and click "Search domain".

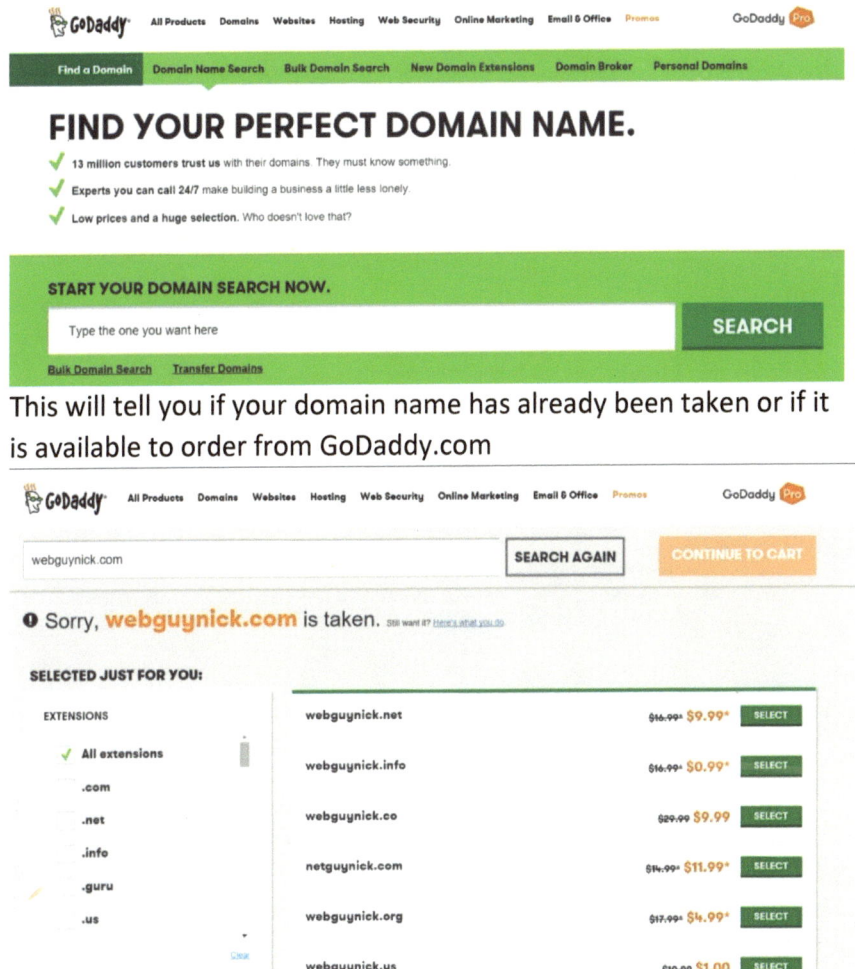

This will tell you if your domain name has already been taken or if it is available to order from GoDaddy.com

1. Selecting a Domain.

Click Select and Continue to Cart.

Once at the Cart, you will be offered a number of options including Hosting packages, Email and Privacy options. In order to have a self-hosted WordPress site, you will need to purchase hosting at this time.

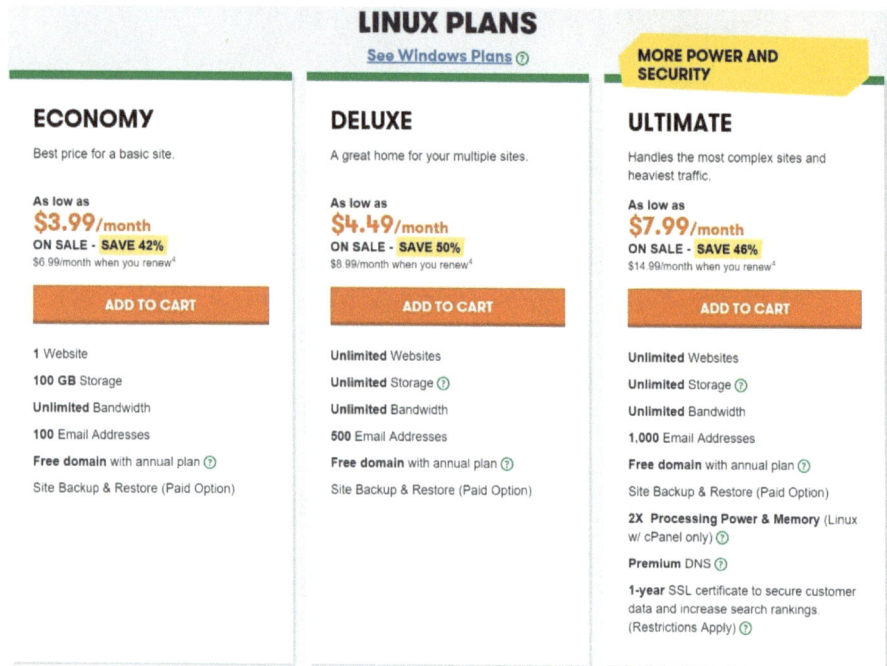

Alternatively Godaddy.com invariably always has a series of offers going on at any time. Sometimes this means that if you purchase your hosting first, you will be given a free domain name with your purchase.

2. Selecting a Hosting Package

2. Selecting a Hosting Package

What is Hosting?

A web hosting service is a type of Internet hosting service that allows individuals and organizations to make their website accessible via the World Wide Web.

Web hosts are companies that provide space on a server owned or leased for use by clients, as well as providing Internet connectivity, typically in a data center.

Purchasing Hosting on GoDaddy.com

Go to GoDaddy.com.

Click on Hosting in the top Menu Bar or in the Side Bar which states "Web Hosting" and click 'Get Started'.

2. Selecting a Hosting Package

There are many different hosting options out there and it can be easily confused when you start seeing Linux Plans & Windows Plans. The basic difference between the two is that a Linux Plan uses a cPanel administrative system and a Windows plan uses PLESK administrative system.

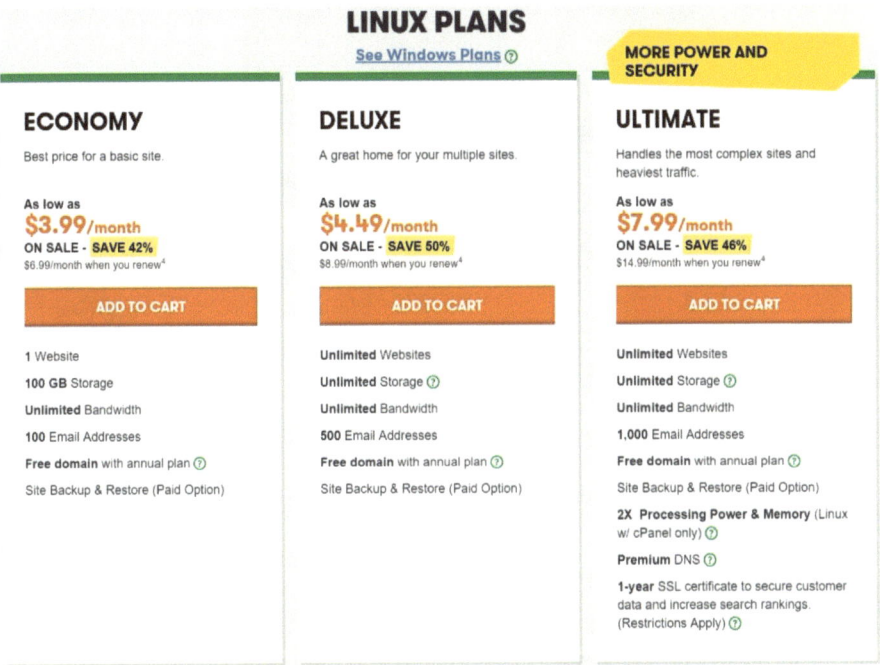

For the purposes of this guide, we will be selecting a basic Linux economy plan which offers a free domain name with it. However choose the plan that works best for your purpose and budget. There are many options available.

2. Selecting a Hosting Package

Once you have selected your plan, it will bring you to another page to search for your domain name. Press Select & Continue.

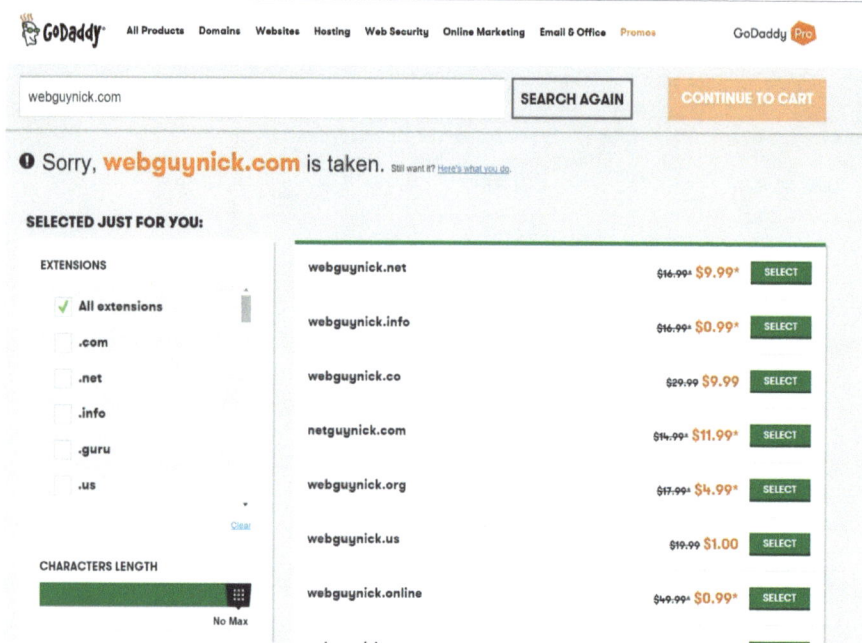

Proceed to checkout, filling out your billing and personal details until it tells you that Payment has been successful and you are ready to proceed to set up your Self-Hosted WordPress Website.

3. WordPress Quick Install

3. WordPress Quick Install

Now you have your domain name and you're hosting! Next you will need to install WordPress to host your website.

Return to your Godaddy.com account and go to Hosting. This will show your domain name and its current status. Click on "Manage". This will open up the cPanel Home Page.

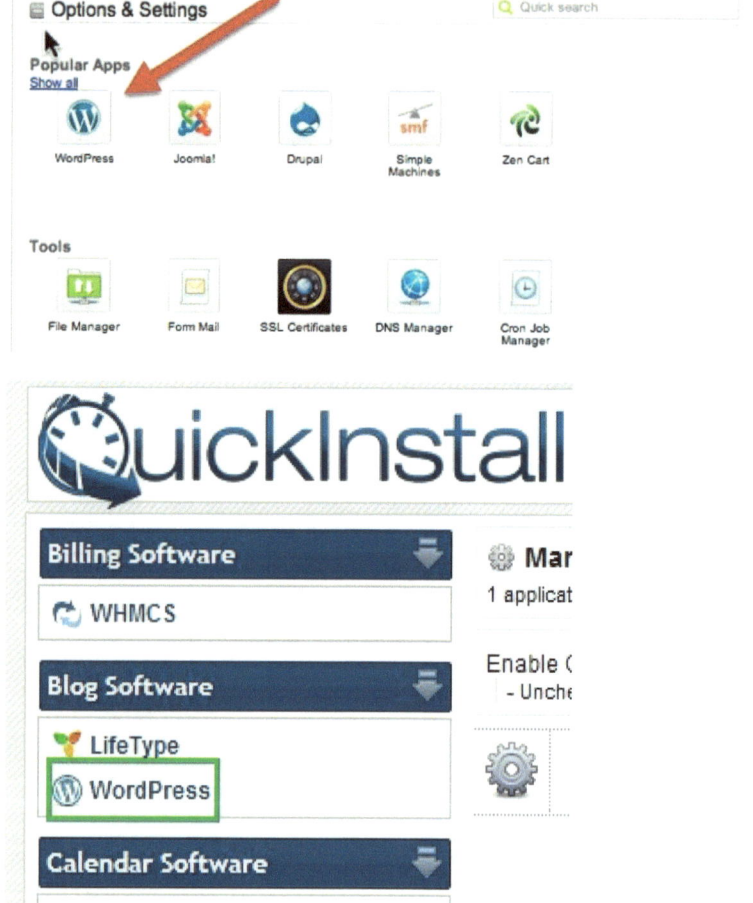

3. WordPress Quick Install

In the cPanel home page, scroll to the Web Applications section, click WordPress blog and click install this application.

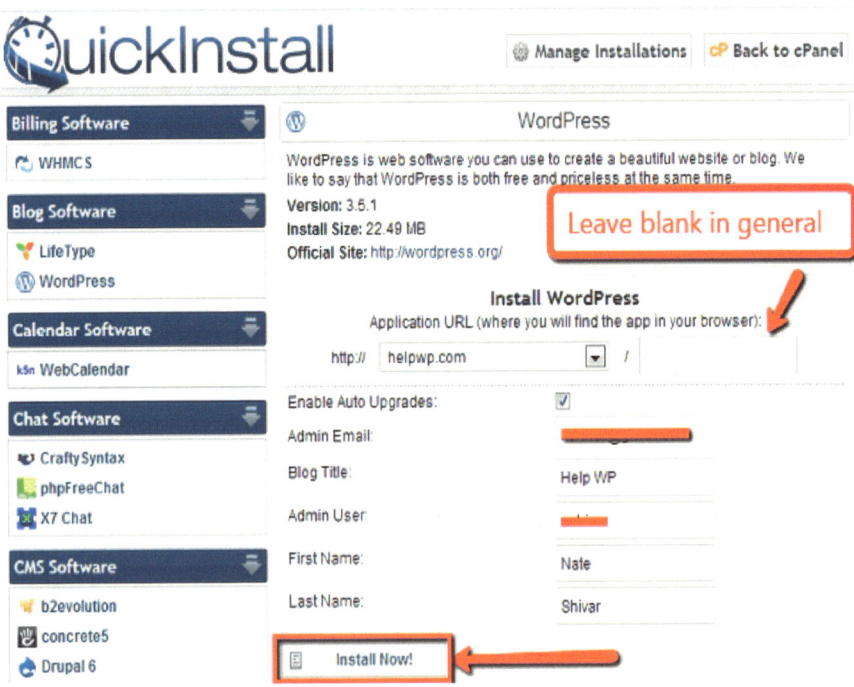

Then select the domain name you want to use. Enter the directory where you want to install WordPress and select the version of WordPress you want to use. Godaddy.com will recommend using all of these default settings

At this stage, there are a number of options here that are automatically generated for you. It's important to note them because they include the username and password you will have to use to log in to your WordPress site. If you are happy you have noted your username and password for WordPress correctly, then click install now.

4. Setting up Your WordPress Site

4. Setting up Your WordPress Site

When you login into your WordPress site for the first time as an administrator, you will invariably enter as the Administrator using the web address which is sent to you after the WordPress installation.

Usually, this takes the form of www.yourdomain.com/wp-admin/

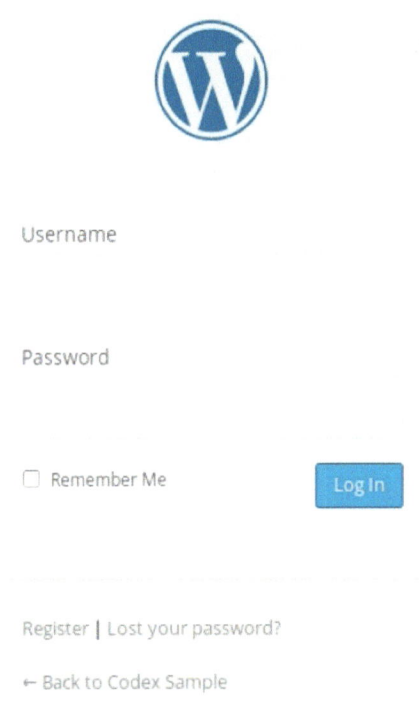

Username

Password

☐ Remember Me   Log In

Register | Lost your password?

← Back to Codex Sample

This will bring you to a login screen where you will enter the details you took note of earlier.

4. Setting up Your WordPress Site

When you get in, you will be in the WordPress Dashboard as shown below.

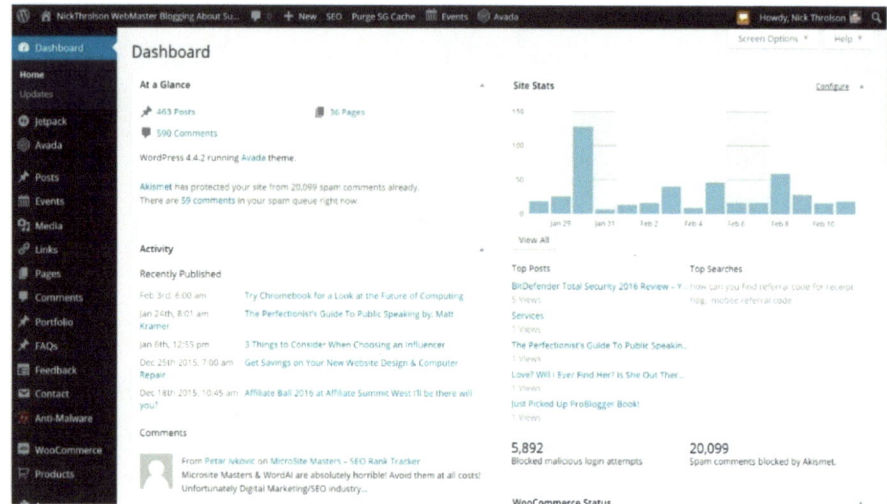

For More Information & Tutorials about the WordPress dashboard.
Visit: http://www.wpbeginner.com/category/beginners-guide/

www.wpbeginner.com

4. Setting up Your WordPress Site

Publishing Your First Page

To get started adding a new page to your WordPress site, find the Pages menu in the WordPress Dashboard Navigation menu.

Click Add new. Add the title of the page, like about. Next, add some content.

The Publish section of the page editor is exactly the same as for writing posts. When you're ready to publish, you can either publish immediately, save this or a draft, or schedule the page to be published later.

The Page Attributes section applies a parent page and template to your new page. For the Parent section, you can arrange your pages into hierarchies. For example, you could create this new page with additional pages under it. There are no limits to how many levels you can nest pages.

The Order box allows you to order your page numerically. Pages are usually ordered alphabetically, but you can choose your own order by entering a number in this field.

Preview the page one last time, then click Publish. You've added a new page to your WordPress site. Repeat the above steps to set up a Page for Contact Info, About Me.

5. What's your niche?

5. What's your niche?

Finding the right niche can be very difficult for some of us, so I want to share with you 10 tips to finding the right niche:

1. Consider your interests: It's considerably easier to keep churning out great content if you're genuinely interested in the niche that you're writing about!

2. Interests don't just mean hobbies: That doesn't just mean your hobbies. You can write about your favorite sports team or even your career!

3. Think about your target demographic: The niche you pick will impact the kind of person who will read your content.

4. Consider fan sites: A fan site is a niche with a dedicated and passionate niche!

5. Think about the content: Is content for your niche going to be forthcoming? Are there lots of news? Will your articles be evergreen?

5. What's your niche?

6. Check out the competition: See what's already there to get an idea of whether that niche is potentially profitable. One tool I use for this is Spyfu.com

7. Avoid saturated markets: This is the main problem with fitness or the make money niche. Use the suggestions we've covered to avoid direct competition!

8. Think how your niche will affect your tone: Do you want a light-hearted, conversational site? Or a serious, technical one?

9. Consider learning a new subject: If there is no niche you know inside out, consider learning one! You can write about it as you write, people love to see progress. You can learn a new course with Udemy or Coursera

10. Think of your business model ahead of time: Know how you plan to Make money before you go ahead, as your niche will greatly impact your plan!

Ultimately be creative! There is more than one niche! Be creative to find your groove and your website will be much more fun to run and much more profitable.

6. Who is your audience?

6. Who is your audience?

How do you establish who your audience in your writing is? Start with these four questions:

Question One: Theme

Think about your stories, posts, tweets, emails, conversations, Facebook statuses, and Instagram pictures. What theme does your writing have in common? As you look at your writing, you will hopefully see a theme. Most people will spot a very specific topic, niche, or theme that their posts, layout, tweets reveal.

Question Two: Demographics

What demographic does my theme appeal to? The theme that you've established will likely have a type of person it appeals to, and this type person can often be defined by demographics. Demographics can also be defined by specific hobbies or interests a person has, for example, writing, ballet, painting, hiking, or food.

6. Who is your audience?

Question Three: Daily Concerns

What are their daily concerns? If you were able to answer the first two questions, you have almost established your audience (and get back to writing!).But now you need to know them on a deeper level. What are their daily preoccupations? Do they struggle with writing? Are they overwhelmed with kids? Do they want to know how to eat healthier?

A great and simple way to find this out is to simply ask. Send out a survey to your email list. Find out what people want.

Question Four: You're Contribution

You've established who your audience will be, and now you're going to offer your experience and expertise. This is where you are able to establish the relationship and build trust. How can you help? How will you help?

The reality is that when you know who you're talking to, your prose, vocabulary, and style will change. This is a good thing because you're figuring out how to write in such a way that it has a deep and lasting impact on their lives.

7. Social Media Optimization and integration with WordPress posts.

7. Social Media Optimization and integration with WordPress posts.

There are many SMO tools and options out there for your website. So much so I could dedicate another eBook to just SMO in WordPress alone! So for this reason, I will give you this advice when it comes to SMO I don't purpose to spend too long.

1. Decide which Social Media Outlets you wish to showcase.

2. Go to https://wordpress.org/plugins/search.php?q=social+media

3. Match Your Preferences to those available.

4. Follow the instructions for installing the Plugin on your dashboard.

Recommended WordPress Plugins

www.OptinMonster.com *"Best Email Opt in Form Plugin"*

www.WooCommerce.com *"Sell Stuff on your WordPress site with this simple plug-in"*

Don't have time to build your own website?

If you would like more information or do not have the time to build a website for yourself please visit www.NickThrolson.com/free-quote/ I would be more than happy to have me and my team work on any size project.

Websites Designed By Nick Throlson

www.PaulJFoster.com

www.JoeRodriguez.co

www.TextBookProfessor.com

www.ForgottenWizard.com

www.Williedjr.com

Websites Designed By Nick Throlson At Allegra Marketing Print Mail

www.LifeTimeFenceSupply.com

www.PetesRS.com

www.HulseyContracting.com

www.RiversideRegionAdulted.org

www.RoyalRanges.com

I would have never written this book alone get it done if it was not for Synergy Master Mind a group started by Joe Rodriguez a Motivational Speaker who is living his dream. I thank Joe Rodriguez , Al Batinga, Matt Kramer aka TacticalTalks.com, Willie Davis Jr. Mary Houmes, Dave Ireland, Paul Foster & Maria Fregoso.

This book is dedicated to my Sister Rebecca Schuurmans love you sis nothing but success in your years to come!

Website Notes

WEBSITE NOTES

WEBSITE NOTES

WEBSITE NOTES

WEBSITE NOTES

WEBSITE NOTES

WEBSITE NOTES

WEBSITE NOTES

WEBSITE NOTES

WEBSITE NOTES

WEBSITE NOTES